THE GOD ASSIGNMENT

THE GOD ASSIGNMENT

ACKNOWLEDGE VOLUME 1

DUANE CHAPMAN

ISBN-13: 978-1500992309

ISBN-10: 1500992305

To my wife, Carla, my son, Nation, and those I am assigned to.

My God, cause us to dream again.

Foreword

Duane's witness is complex. He has a passion for Jesus Christ that shows itself as compassion for those who are lost or hurting, and a worship-filled heart. He is over-the-top with enthusiasm for helping others find and live God's purpose for their lives. God gives Duane insight so that he sees behaviors, but does not identify them as cemented personality traits. People are drawn to him because of this gift. Combine Duane's God-loving heart, depth of insight, and conviction with the great capacity he has for marshalling his human energy, and this book is one result.

Duane and I spent many hours on phone conversations over the years – a habit we formed when he was a teen-man. Back then, God often allowed me to phone at odd times and find Duane home, alone. He became confident that he could ask me any question, with respect, and express freely teen-adult emotions and frustrations. During one of those heated conversations, I asked Duane to pray and ask God to reveal Himself and His plan to Duane, personally. The rest is His-story. I've since learned that some of the conversations Duane and I shared occurred at crucial or pivotal decision-making moments in his life. God used my chatty behavior to send His son, Duane, some wise words that he could use to help him make Godly decisions.

I once asked Duane what he thought about *how* our conversations unfolded. I mused, "I wonder why we don't talk like this when we meet face-to-face?" His reply is typical of teen-adults, "I can just talk better when I don't have to look at the other person." That understanding of others, leads to this book's format. This book is written in Duane's own speaking voice, and in his own writing style. He writes each segment as briefly as his intended message will allow, mirroring his knowledge that his audience prefers shorter messages. He uses vivid illustrations and examples, finding some in scripture and pulling others from his own life experiences.

Today, as you read, know that God is using Duane to send some loving and wise words to you. These words are in Duane's voice, but they are from God's heart. Listen. Obey. Live. I pray that you will, like Duane, mature spiritually. May these words from God via Duane help you on your journey in God's purpose.

Lillie R. Jenkins (a.k.a., Aunt P.)

January 17, 2013

Preface

As long as I can remember I always liked to see people happy. I would use every effort I could to ensure that everyone I came in contact with felt loved. At the time, I was not sure why I did these things; it just came natural. As I got older I realized that not only do I want to see people happy, but I wanted them to be hopeful in life as well. Hopeful in life to me includes understanding that you are made on purpose with a specific purpose. That purpose is what I refer to as an assignment. So no matter where you are in the world or what you've done or how insignificant you may feel, your assignment is still on the inside of you waiting for you to find it. A bird finds a way to fly whether they are in the small town of Montezuma or the large metropolis of Los Angeles. <u>Don't die without seeing the genius in you work</u>! I hate to see young men and young women slaughtering themselves in the streets. I believe if they knew they had a purpose they would think twice before putting themselves in a dangerous position. I hate to see my brothers and sisters in the body of Christ sitting on the side lines of life. For as we use the gifts and talents on the inside of us, we edify (strengthen, encourage) the other members of the body to use their gifting. We then all get closer to fulfilling our *God Assignment* which in turn will make the earth a much better place. That's what these series of devotionals are about. Helping you first to <u>acknowledge</u>, then <u>find</u>, and finally <u>finish</u> your assignment. **The most effective way to read this book is to focus on one page per day**. Really think about what it is saying and take some time to look at the scriptures for yourself. I pray you come to know God through his son Jesus, and the incredible assignment he has just for you!

The First Step

Matthew 3:16

16And Jesus, when he was baptized, went up straightway out of the water: and, lo, the heavens were opened unto him, and he saw the Spirit of God descending like a dove, and lighting upon him:

Accepting Jesus into your heart and being baptized is the door to your Kingdom assignment. It is the door to your new world/future. Can you fulfill your *divine* assignment outside the Kingdom of God? Nope! You can only do part of it because it is spiritually discerned. You will never know the peace or the true success God has planned for you because you are following your own plan to fulfill your assignment.

Your purpose was spoken and decreed into the world before you were born. Follow the God given path and be as little children; get excited about doing those things that make your parents pleased.

Reference Scriptures:

James 1:17

Colossians 3:3, 10

II Corinthians 5:17

Notes

Don't Be Robbed of Your Promise

Hebrews 4:11-12

[11]Let us labor therefore to enter into that rest, lest any man fall after the same example of unbelief.

[12]For the word of God is quick, and powerful, and sharper than any two-edged sword, piercing even to the dividing asunder of soul and spirit, and of the joints and marrow, and is a discerner of the thoughts and intents of the heart.

The story leading up to these particular passages describes how God made the children of Israel a promise that they would enter into the land he had prepared for them. Because it was reported there were giants in the land, the children of Israel became fearful and unwilling to fight to enter that land. As a result, that particular generation missed out on the absolute best plan that God had for their lives.

Let the above scriptures be both a warning and a motivation directing you to labor (use speed, give diligence, study) and fight the good fight of faith so you may enter into that rest. "Rest" is the picture of the assignment that God has shown you; the place prepared for you (see Deuteronomy 11:11-12). For the word that God speaks is living, full of power and unstoppable. He just requires you to believe it, act on it, and *fight off every voice* that tries to tell you that you cannot accomplish God's assigned will for your life!

Reference Scriptures:

Jeremiah 29:11 (See the Message Translation)

II Corinthians 1:20

Notes

Born with Purpose

Jeremiah 1:5

⁵Before I formed thee in the belly I knew thee; and before thou camest forth out of the womb I sanctified thee, and I ordained thee a prophet unto the nations.

Before you were formed in your mother's womb, God knew you. This means he was well informed on how he made you, what family you would go to, what environment you would thrive in, etc. Understand this truth, our parents/those in charge of us may have made wrong life decisions that for a time negatively affected God's perfect plan for our lives. <u>We also</u> might have made some destiny altering choices.

Before you were born into the earth your purpose had already been assigned by God. Look at what angers you, what you naturally gravitate towards, what subjects get you excited. Above all, seek the one that put the purpose in you.

<u>Reference Scriptures:</u>

I Timothy 4:14-15

Acts 17:26-27

Ephesians 2:10 (also see the Amplified Version)

Notes

So Easy

Philippians 2:13

¹³For it is God which worketh in you both to will and to do of his good pleasure.

There is a work working in you which is not your own. This purpose, this desire, is of God and God alone. **He** is the motivation for it, **he** reveals it to you, and **he** causes you to love and long after that particular purpose.

Not only is he proving that he needs you, but he is working in you to reveal your purpose, to help you delight in the purpose. He is also providing the energy and strength to fulfill it. That's good news because all that's left for you to do is just follow him.

Remember, your assignment is God's good pleasure.

Reference Scriptures:

Hebrews 13:21

Colossians 1:29 (His working –working in the Greek language means energy, thus it's His energy!)

Notes

More than You

Philippians 2:4

⁴Look not every man on his own things, but every man also on the things of others.

A lot of people assume that they should use their gifts to benefit themselves only but according to this verse, your assignment includes helping others be successful as well. God wants to use you in such a way that others may be stirred up to fulfill and/or continue their God-given callings.

True success is not measured by how great you have become but by the number of people you helped and motivated to achieve their God-given dreams. Nobody becomes successful by themselves. Other people believe in us, pray for us, mentor us, or invest in our lives in other ways. Jesus set the ultimate example by leaving the glorious life he lived in heaven to come to earth and live in the form of a man, die a horrible death, so that we might live.

As representatives of Christ, not only is it our duty to help others, but we have been given the necessary equipment to do it.

Reference Scriptures:

I Corinthians 10:24

Esther 10:3

I Timothy 6: 18

Notes

He wants you to know

Ephesians 1:9

⁹Having made known unto us the mystery of his will, according to his good pleasure which he hath purposed in himself.

Don't fall into the trap thinking that your life's purpose is impossible to find. According to this verse, it is God's pleasure to make known unto us His will.

Normally people fall short when we do not <u>consistently</u> seek God (or we do not seek him at all!). Seeking God is just like spending time with a friend. We spend time with God in order to become more familiar with him and to gain insight on his plan for our lives. We must remember that our **true** lives are hidden in Christ, so Christ is the door to discovering what is inside us.

Take a new cell phone for example. When you purchase a new phone, it comes with an owner's manual that describes all functions. Now, most of us don't look at the owner's guide. We would rather just push buttons and find out how it works by ourselves. While that may be one way of doing it, imagine how much more quickly we could have learned the functions of our phones if we would have spent time reading the instructions. In the past I have had a cell phone for months before I realized its capabilities.

Unfortunately, this example shows how most people live their lives. Full of great abilities, but slowly or never discovering them because they will not spend time seeking the One who made them, and can tell them how to use their abilities best. Just as cellphones have a certain life expectancy, we do too! Don't waste time trying one thing after another. Seek God for your purpose. He wants you to know!

Reference Scriptures:

Romans 8:32

Psalms 32:8

Isaiah 30:21

Notes

_____
_____
_____
_____
_____
_____
_____
_____
_____
_____
_____
_____
_____
_____
_____
_____
_____
_____
_____
_____
_____
_____
_____
_____
_____
_____
_____
_____

Making His Paths Straight

Matthew 3:3

3For this is he that was spoken of by the prophet Esaias, saying, The voice of one crying in the wilderness, Prepare ye the way of the Lord, make his paths straight.

In this verse we see the manifestation of a prophetic word spoken by Esaias. John the Baptist had now been born and come into his predestined role of preparing the way for Jesus' ministry by preaching, baptizing and calling people to repent.

Just as God used John as a vessel to "make way" for the introduction of Jesus, God uses us and our assignments, talents, gifts, and purposes that we may also be sources for introducing Jesus and Kingdom concepts to the world. Understand this, as children of God we have become *partners* with God. He gives us everything in abundance to "clear a path" for him to walk straight into a person's life.

Reference Scriptures:

II Timothy 2:20-21 (Also See Message Translation)

Luke 1:76

Luke 9:52

Notes

Push Past Temptations

Matthew 4:1,17

[1]Then was Jesus led up of the Spirit into the wilderness to be tempted of the devil.

[17]From that time Jesus began to preach, and to say, Repent: for the kingdom of heaven is at hand.

Jesus was led into the wilderness by the Holy Spirit to be tempted by **the devil**. I want to state clearly that Jesus was not tempted by God (see James 1:13).

I believe the Holy Spirit led Jesus to be tempted in the wilderness because Jesus was not used to walking in accordance to the flesh. He had to experience this for our sake to be better acquainted with the temptations we face. If it was not for the leading of the Holy Spirit, I do not believe Jesus would have put himself in a position to be tempted.

Think of the impact it would have had if Jesus gave in to the temptations. In the first two temptations (read Matthew 4:1-11), we read that Satan was trying to see if Jesus was really the son of God. If Jesus would have given in and validated who he was prematurely, Satan would have made sure Jesus was never crucified and, as a result, there would be no sacrifice appropriate for our complete salvation.

The last temptation was for the kingdoms of the world. If Jesus would have bowed down to Satan and worshiped him for the kingdoms, then he would have become Satan's slave.

Yielding to temptations will prevent you from fulfilling your assignment; it will stop you from impacting the lives of people you are meant to touch for good. If you have yielded (as we all have at some point), repent and go forward. There are people that need you!

Reference Scriptures:

Numbers 20:7-12

Psalm 40:12-17

Notes

_____
_____
_____
_____
_____
_____
_____
_____
_____
_____
_____
_____
_____
_____
_____
_____
_____
_____
_____
_____
_____
_____
_____
_____
_____
_____
_____
_____
_____

Enjoying Your Purpose

Isaiah 65:22

22They shall not build, and another inhabit; they shall not plant, and another eat: for as the days of a tree are the days of my people, and mine elect shall long enjoy the work of their hands.

Often, contrary to your belief, the assignment God has called you to is meant to be long-lasting, enjoyable, and profitable. In the past, it was assumed that when God called you to do something it would be something you would hate. Unfortunately, a lot of the people who were teaching this ideology were standing in teaching positions where God had not called them to stand.

According to Isaiah 65:22, God wants you to enjoy your work. It is He who has created you to do the work. He has put the gifts, talents, and the assignment on the inside of you. Your assignment will be along the same lines as those things he has placed in you; things that you probably like doing already!

Reference Scripture:
Ecclesiastes 5:19-20

Notes

Solomon-Type Success

I Kings 3:9-11

[9]Give therefore thy servant an understanding heart to judge thy people, that I may discern between good and bad: for who is able to judge this thy so great a people?

[10]And the speech pleased the Lord, that Solomon had asked this thing.

[11]And God said unto him, Because thou hast asked this thing, and hast not asked for thyself long life; neither hast asked riches for thyself, nor hast asked the life of thine enemies; but hast asked for thyself understanding to discern judgment;

In this scripture Solomon was given an opportunity to ask God for anything! Instead of making a request for more power, territory, or money, Solomon asked for the thing that would help him fulfill his God-given assignment (being a king) with excellence. The next verse says that God was so pleased with Solomon's request that he also released incredible things that Solomon did not ask for.

Our purpose could have been given to anyone, but God placed it in us. We should determine to take *our* assignments seriously and take every opportunity to develop and grow them to maturity. That type of attitude pleases God and blesses you abundantly.

Reference Scriptures:

1 Samuel 2:30b

Proverbs 8:17-21

Notes

Am I Necessary?

I Corinthians 9:16

¹⁶For though I preach the gospel, I have nothing to glory of: for necessity is laid upon me; yea, woe is unto me, if I preach not the gospel!

Assignments come from a desire of God to have something done in the earth. What a privilege it is to be selected for use by the Creator of all things!

Notice even in our everyday surroundings the purpose of different things. Grass provides a beautiful, green carpet for the earth and holds in moisture to keep the ground refreshed. Trees release oxygen. Sand is used in making glass, cement, and many other things. Everything God has made was made for a good purpose! If we can clearly see this, then we should be able to clearly see how *necessary* we are to God's plan.

Paul did not recognize his true assignment at first either, but he had an "eye opening" encounter with God that caused him to realize *his true purpose*. When he realized and acknowledged his purpose, it became necessary for him to do it. Paul came to understand what he was created to do and that no other occupation would satisfy him.

I don't know where you are in this point of your life. I don't know your past, but I do know that you were designed for something only you can do. It will bring you such joy and fulfillment that you will gladly let go of your old way of life. If you desire that fulfilled life – that life of recognized purpose – just ask the Heavenly Father to open your eyes to it. Then, simply follow what He shows you.

Reference Scriptures:

Ephesians 1:18

Proverbs 16:4 (see Message Translation)

Notes

Don't Be A Sluggard

Proverbs 15:19

[19]The way of the slothful man is as an hedge of thorns: but the way of the righteous is made plain.

Your assignment will require consistent, daily work. You will be elevated to a new level in your assignment as you give yourself more and more to the work. It is the principal of being faithful in the small opportunities and, as a result, you will be advanced to greater ones. Not only that, but as you pursue the first step of your vision, the next step becomes even clearer.

Remember, to be truly skillful in your assignment you must give yourself to it!

Reference Scriptures:

Hebrews 6:11-12

II Timothy 2:15

Judges 18:10

Notes

Change Your Mind

Romans 12:2

²And be not conformed to this world: but be ye transformed by the renewing of your mind, that ye may prove what is that good, and acceptable, and perfect, will of God.

What God has called you to be may be nothing like the way the world, or maybe even your family, sees you. One sure way to manifest the unique person God created you to be is to meditate and think on God's Word. This allows you to <u>think on His thoughts</u>!

Listening to His thoughts about you consistently can take you from being a depressed drug addict to living the life of a billionaire businessman; doing good works for the kingdom. Listening to His thoughts about you *consistently* will take you from being in a hopeless state to testifying that there is hope.

To reach that untapped greatness – the treasure hidden in you – you must change your thoughts!

<u>Reference Scriptures:</u>

Colossians 3:2-3

Ephesians 4:23

Notes

Different But Connected For Growth

Romans 12:4-6

⁴For as we have many members in one body, and all members have not the same office:

⁵So we, being many, are one body in Christ, and every one members one of another.

⁶Having then gifts differing according to the grace that is given to us, whether prophecy, let us prophesy according to the proportion of faith;

God uses the example of a human body and all its different parts to explain how Christians can all be like members of the same body, but have different assignments, gifts, and callings. The goal is the same, but each of us may be used in a different capacity as we work together to reach that goal.

Points to Consider

- The talents you have are from God, placed in you for His good pleasure.
- Acknowledging the gifts is just the first step.
- You can only use your gift based on your faith in and knowledge of it. The more you give yourself to it, the greater it will become!
- Don't be ashamed to start where you are.
- As *you* grow and develop, you are helping the body of Christ grow and develop all the more!

Reference Scriptures:

I Corinthians 12:4-6, 18

Mark 3:25

Notes

Not So Fast!

Jeremiah 1:12

[12]Then said the Lord unto me, Thou hast well seen: for I will hasten my word to perform it.

That word in you (your purpose spoken by God) has a specific time for it to come into existence. We may be in a hurry to manifest the vision, but it is not our job to try to bring it about speedily.

I have had to remind myself about this on several occasions. Over the years, I have begun to learn some of the things God has gifted me to do, and I have tried at the wrong times to pursue ventures and use those gifts. This wrongly timed pursuit usually ended in failure which was followed by *self-created discouragement*. I've learned that instead of trying to make something happen, **I just *prepare myself* for the opportunity**!

I encourage you to do the same. Go to school if need be. Find a mentor that's doing what you would love to do. Read literature on your passion. Write the books in your heart, or produce the songs in your mind. Then **let God** bring you to the forefront when He's ready.

Reference Scriptures:

Luke 1:20b

Luke 1:80

Notes

How to Gain Access

Proverbs 18:16

[16]A man's gift maketh room for him, and bringeth him before great men.

God has designed it that the earth will make room for you as you begin to walk in your gifts and assignment. In fact, once you begin to operate in your assignment and gifts, people will begin to give you access to their lives.

For instance, when Michael Jordan began to walk in his gifting as a basketball player, he became a household name. Even years after his retirement, people are still lining up to purchase his brand of sneakers. When Bill Gates found his gift working with and designing computers, people all over the world gave him access to their lives by purchasing the software and technology he had created. We could go on and on, listing names of men and women who have found their gifts, pursued them, and now the earth has made room for them.

So be encouraged and know that God has designed a place for you, but you must first find, then walk in that gifting. **The earth will make room for you!**

Reference Scripture:

Proverbs 17:8

Notes

The Kingdom Information System

Job 32:7-9

⁷I said, Days should speak, and multitude of years should teach wisdom.

⁸But there is a spirit in man: and the inspiration of the Almighty giveth them understanding.

⁹Great men are not always wise: neither do the aged understand judgment.

The first thing I would like to point out is in verse 8 of this passage. It says "the inspiration of the Almighty giveth them understanding," which means your purpose (among other things) is meant to be revealed to your inner man by the Spirit of God.

With this in mind we can now understand that it is the Spirit of God that reveals to us what our profession is supposed to be. Once this is revealed, we can then pursue the right avenue to develop in that profession; be it college, trade school, intern/apprentice, etc.

We have been taught in our society to first finish high school, then go to college and pursue a degree that will make us a bunch of money or that will be usable in the years to come. While this may make "*good sense*," what usually follows after applying this "knowledge" is we end up with a large society of out-of-place, unfulfilled people. We must not neglect the information system of heaven which provides us accurate and timely information in turn, causing us to perform at a level beyond our peers or the most intellectual. God has provided so that **His children** can know His perfect will for their lives!

Reference Scriptures:

Daniel 1:17, 20

I Corinthians 2:10

Notes

From You to Them

Hebrews 6:7

⁷For the earth which drinketh in the rain that cometh oft upon it, and bringeth forth herbs meet for them by whom it is dressed, receiveth blessing from God:

Soil is made to "drink" rain and produce crops. Fish are made to swim. Ants are made to colonize and gather food. You are made to do something specific too! In fact, when you begin doing the thing you were created to do, two things will happen.

First, you will bring pleasure to the creator of all Heaven and Earth and, as a result, he will ensure you are even more fruitful/ profitable. Second, you will notice that you become a source of encouragement for others. You will, at this point, begin to know and enjoy the fulfillment of life that so many people are searching for.

Remember, when you are doing <u>what</u> God has called you to do and <u>how</u> he has called you to do it, you are capable of blessing others and bringing blessings upon yourself.

<u>Reference Scripture:</u>

II Timothy 2:21 (see Amplified and Message Translation)

Notes

It Will Stand

Proverbs 19:21 (AMP)

²¹Many plans are in a man's mind, But it is the Lord's purpose for him that will stand (be carried out).

There are many external things fighting for your undivided attention, as well as the many thoughts and plans stirring deep within you. With all of this going on, how do you find the right focus? According to this scripture, only the counsel of the Lord will stand.

What you will discover as you advance in life is that those things you thought you would be doing begin to fade away. But if you pay close attention, you will find that one thing or things that no circumstance could displace.

Reference Scriptures:

Philippians 1:6

I Thessalonians 5:21

Notes

He Opens the Door

Revelation 3:7-8

⁷And to the angel of the church in Philadelphia write; These things saith he that is holy, he that is true, he that hath the key of David, he that openeth, and no man shutteth; and shutteth, and no man openeth;

⁸I know thy works: behold, I have set before thee an open door, and no man can shut it: for thou hast a little strength, and hast kept my word, and hast not denied my name.

The Word of God will open your mind to concepts and ideas most people cannot believe. It has the power in itself to keep your mind open, believing even when others see things as impossible.

One of the great things about God is that he understands the limitations of man, yet he still desires to do great things for and through us. It is His job to open the doors of "impossibility" for us, while it is our job to obey His word.

Obeying His word and not denying Jesus supersedes your lack of qualifications, even your lack of education!

Reference Scripture:

John 7:15

Notes

<u>Accept It</u>

Romans 11:29

²⁹For the gifts and calling of God are without repentance.

Don't get caught up in measuring yourself with the performance of someone else. This type of analyzing will cause you to miss, neglect, or possibly reject the calling of God on the inside of you. Satan's pleasure is to try to do things that will make you devalue the gifts that God has placed in you so that you would have no desire to see them fulfilled. Do not allow the enemy to con you out of your purpose!

God will not change his mind about what he has graced you to do. **You** will be held accountable for wasting such divine greatness. Accept who you truly are, *for God's gifts on the inside of you are presents to bless the world.*

Reference Scripture:

I Corinthians 12:18

Notes

<u>Beyond The Mind</u>

I Corinthians 1:27

[27]But God hath chosen the foolish things of the world to confound the wise; and God hath chosen the weak things of the world to confound the things which are mighty;

Your assignment must be spiritually discerned! The reason for this is because God will do things and call us to do things that may not "make sense."

It seems foolish to call a man to speak that has a speech impediment. It seems foolish to call a young boy with a slingshot and a few rocks to fight a 9 foot tall giant wearing armor of up to 200lbs. It seems foolish to instruct a man to sow seed into land that was void of moisture and no rain or irrigation systems in sight.

Stop trying to rationalize your assignment. God is too big to fit in a box. Our brain, even though an incredible organ, is too small to process the vision. God speaks to your **reborn** spirit because your **reborn** spirit comes from eternity and is capable of receiving such great possibilities.

If you try to figure out your assignment with your mind only, you will fail!

<u>Reference Scripture:</u>

Exodus 4

1 Samuel 17

I Corinthians 2

Notes

Faithful is He!

I Thessalonians 5:24

²⁴Faithful is he that calleth you, who also will do it.

My mother died when I was a young teenager. It was a hard thing for me to believe in the greatness and trustworthiness of God when I saw my mom so many times confess the healing word of God and still die. To this day, I have no explanation for why she didn't get better, but I can truly testify to God's faithfulness! See, when I review my life and all the haphazard things I have done, all the drugs, all the cigarettes, all the stupid decisions I made in the past, I can clearly see His faithfulness.

My mom and many other family members prayed for me to be a man of God, and here it is years later after all the foolish things I did; I am alive living out the manifestations of those prayers. That, my friend, is faithfulness!

Things happen sometimes that we can't explain, but remember, God cannot change. He will always be faithful!

Reference Scriptures:

Lamentations 3:22-23

Psalms 36:5

Notes

Give Yourself To It

Acts 6:4

⁴But we will give ourselves continually to prayer, and to the ministry of the word.

Did you know that it's been reported that you need to spend at least 10,000 hours doing something before you master it? [1]

You've probably heard the story how Bill Gates averaged a total of 10,000 hours programming computers and how the Beatles before their fame, played a total of 10,000 hours. So too, Joseph in the bible spent years in preparation to be second in command. Even Jesus took several years to prepare for his purpose.

The point is this; you must first recognize your life's purpose, then you must master it (understanding of course, there is always more to learn). Once you master it, you prove you are ready to take your place.

Reference Scriptures:
I Samuel 17:33-37
Esther 2:12

[1] Donahue, Deirdre (2008-11-18). "Malcom Gladwell's 'Success' defines 'outlier' achievement." *USA Today*. Retrieved 2009-01-12.

Notes

Serve Your Gift

I Peter 4:10-11

[10]As every man hath received the gift, even so minister the same one to another, as good stewards of the manifold grace of God.

[11]If any man speak, let him speak as the oracles of God; if any man minister, let him do it as of the ability which God giveth: that God in all things may be glorified through Jesus Christ, to whom be praise and dominion for ever and ever. Amen.

These verses were so power-packed with revelations that it seemed easier to just list a few of them. Enjoy!

- Your gifts are an expression of the manifold grace of God in you.
- The grace (charis) of God is a gift (charisma) to us. That gift in us is to be used as a gift, first to the Body of Christ, then to the world. In verse 10, the Greek work for grace is "charis." The Greek word for gift is "charisma," which happens to be the same place we get the English word *charisma*. Look at the definition of Charisma: (n) 1. Compelling attractiveness or charm that can inspire devotion in others; 2. A <u>Divinely conferred</u> power of talent.
- One way to recognize your gifts is that when in operation it should bring joy, delight, and encouragement to another.
- We are in error if we know the gifts of God in us and are not using them to serve one another.
- Your gifts have been packed with the supernatural ability to supply something someone is needing.
- Your gifts have been supernaturally charged. The level of expression and manifestation of them should be so great that it causes God to be glorified.
- Every man (person) has received the grace!

Notes

Find Your Place

Acts 17:26-27

26And hath made of one blood all nations of men for to dwell on all the face of the earth, and hath determined the times before appointed, and the bounds of their habitation;

27That they should seek the Lord, if haply they might feel after him, and find him, though he be not far from every one of us:

You are designed for a specific time and place. The spiritual atmosphere of that place responds to a specific set of guidelines or rules that are already predetermined. When these rules (God's commands) are followed, you will see the mighty increase in the natural.

Understand this truth: *You can be doing all the right things in the wrong place and you will not succeed.* Take for instance a fish trying to swim in the grass. He may be doing all the correct moves needed to gracefully glide in the sea, but because he is not in the water he will not succeed in his endeavor.

Your success has a place; you must find your place!

Reference Scriptures:

Deuteronomy 1:33

Isaiah 48:17

Notes

Obey!

Deuteronomy 6:18-19

18And thou shalt do that which is right and good in the sight of the Lord: that it may be well with thee, and that thou mayest go in and possess the good land which the Lord sware unto thy fathers,

19To cast out all thine enemies from before thee, as the Lord hath spoken.

Obedience. This is one thing most of us have an issue with. According to this verse, "not doing what is right and good in the sight of God," will prevent three things from happening in your life;

1) **Things going well with you.** This is God making everything in your life sweet!

2) **Possessing the good land.** There is a land filled with *God's best* for you. Disobedience not only keeps you out of the land, but you most certainly will not be able to dominate it!

3) **God casting out all your enemies from before thee.** God is saying that *He* will personally remove the "giants" that war to keep you out of the land. Enemies that are trying to stop your progression, your God expression, your divine possession!

Obedience is the key to fulfilling your assignment!

Reference Scripture:
Numbers 20:7-12

Notes

The Rewards of Fulfilling Your Assignment

Hebrews 12:1-3

¹Wherefore seeing we also are compassed about with so great a cloud of witnesses, let us lay aside every weight, and the sin which doth so easily beset us, and let us run with patience the race that is set before us,

²Looking unto Jesus the author and finisher of our faith; who for the joy that was set before him endured the cross, despising the shame, and is set down at the right hand of the throne of God.

³For consider him that endured such contradiction of sinners against himself, lest ye be wearied and faint in your minds.

There is a race, a path of purpose, set before each one of us. It will take many key elements for us to complete it. Elements including: 1) focus so that we are not distracted by what is going on to the left or to the right, but only what is before us, 2) patience and perseverance so that we don't quit prematurely, and 3) a **constant visualization** of the prize.

The rewards come when you complete each step of your assignment/purpose. Since God has specifically designed the prize to be multifaceted it will include: 1) you reaching and helping the people that you were assigned to, 2) leaving a dynamic legacy in the earth, 4) the wealth and material benefits associated with completing your assignment, and 4) the Father telling you "Well Done," and you entering in and enjoying the eternal rewards in heaven.

The training and the actual race may not be that pleasant, but *winning* at what you were designed to do IS!

Reference Scriptures:
Hebrews 3:14
Psalms 27:13

Notes

Die Empty

Isaiah 55:10-11

10For as the rain cometh down, and the snow from heaven, and returneth not thither, but watereth the earth, and maketh it bring forth and bud, that it may give seed to the sower, and bread to the eater:

11So shall my word be that goeth forth out of my mouth: it shall not return unto me void, but it shall accomplish that which I please, and it shall prosper in the thing whereto I sent it.

The first thing I would like to point out is in verse 10. This verse gives a very good explanation of how we are called to work hand in hand.

The ground could not do its job without the water doing its job. And of course the plant could not come forth and do its job without well watered soil.

The second thing to notice is that God says His word always works. Since His word never fails, the answer for something not producing in our lives is found with us!

Lastly, since our assignment/purpose was spoken into us by God, and His word does not return unto him void, we need to be careful that we fulfill our callings while here on earth. *For dying without fulfilling your purpose is returning to the Lord void!*

Reference Scripture:
Matthew 25:15-30

Notes

Bonus Thoughts

- You not being in the place of assignment may be bringing uncertainty, fear, and trouble to those close to you. (Jonah:1)
- Your gifts/your assignment are from God. He calls them good and he expects them to be used for good. He will not change his mind about what he placed in you. (James 1:17)
- Your assignment is for Kingdom advancement.
- God uses the natural man to do supernatural things.
- No matter how impossible your assignment looks, all you have to do is yield to it. (Luke 1:33, 35, 37-38)
- If you are a mass communications student, in media, movies, music, teacher, etc; this scripture teaches that what comes out of your mouth should be good, Kingdom things that build people up in God's way of thinking. (Ephesians 4:29)
- Wisdom includes understanding God's purpose for your life. (Ephesians 5:17)
- The Word of God contains all the proper instructions to accomplish any task (assignment) with Godly excellence. (II Timothy 3:16-17)
- You were created to solve a problem! (Isaiah 6:8)

<u>Prayer</u>

Father, according to your Word, you have placed every believer into the Body of Christ as it pleased you. We are fearfully and wonderfully made for your pleasure.

Reveal our purposes, our assignments, and gifts to us that we might impact the world, dominate the earth, and show forth your glory. As you manifest our purposes into this earth realm, people will recognize the genius of the *Creator of All Things* and know without a doubt that Jesus is Lord!

Amen.

Made in the USA
Coppell, TX
29 April 2024